ry simple * make them four words * avoid the word
ur coffee black * wear only solid cloth[...]e up
our own tribe * let ot[...]safe
ng and help * let some[...]one
ce * mean what you s[...]in
lighthouse * let yourse[...]urself be
te more love letters * giv[...]one your password *
ices, not things * stop all your whining * fall down,
hood game * be happy in advance * **TRAVEL** * take
talk to your seatmates * get off the highway * tip the
UL * leave some things undone * stop trying so hard
ur tank * say what you can't * turn off the screen *
tretch to stay limber * breathe deeply, and often * let
iner plates * eat more real food * start saying "I can"
* motivate someone to care * always assume positive
* ask why, not how * do something you fear * admit
n earth warrior * watch where you step * turn off the
* buy food from farmers * walk where you can * eat
* take out your earplugs * use your own voice * start
ity * speak up for someone * stop counting, start
espect who they are * give your affection freely *
efrigerator boxes * let kids dress themselves *
an * open doors for others * know what
someone * try on their shoes *
dying * do less, be more * live life
ome * get
* create your four words *

Four-Word Self-Help

{ Simple Wisdom
for Complex Lives }

PATTI DIGH

author of *Life Is a Verb*
and the award-winning blog, *37days*

Guilford, Connecticut
An imprint of Globe Pequot Press

skirt!® is an attitude . . . spirited, independent, outspoken, serious, playful and
irreverent, sometimes controversial, always passionate.

Text design by Sheryl P. Kober
Layout artist Maggie Peterson

Library of Congress Cataloging-in-Publication Data is available on file.

ISBN 978-1-59921-980-6

Printed in China

10 9 8 7 6 5 4 3 2 1

For Daddy,
who was full of simple wisdom

We are here just for a spell and then pass on. So get a few laughs and do the best you can. Live your life so that whenever you lose it, you are ahead.
—WILL ROGERS

contents

*Life is really simple,
but we insist on making it complicated.*
—CONFUCIUS

Why just four words?. VIII

community
Create your own tribe 1

love
Walk hand in hand 15

stress
Jump up and down 27

travel
Take just enough baggage 41

soul
Leave some things undone 53

wellness
Eat less, move more 65

SUCCESS
Do work that matters **77**

GREEN
Be an earth warrior **89**

ACTIVISM
Stand up for something **103**

CHILDREN
Learn from small humans **115**

GENEROSITY
Do what you can **127**

ENDINGS
Live like you're dying. **139**

Create your four words **152**

Meet all the artists **156**

Always say thank you **159**

Who is the author? **160**

DRINK

YOUR

COFFEE

BLACK

WHY JUST FOUR WORDS?

The wisdom of life consists in the elimination of non-essentials.
—LIN YUTANG

A few years ago, I gave up clothing with patterns. Solids only, from that point on. Of course, there are still a few hangers-on—scarves with prints, blouses with swirls of some pseudo-Italian origin like the endpapers of old books—but since that year, I haven't bought clothing except in solid colors, the sartorial equivalent of narrowing my dog food choices to one brand.

Before the clothing simplification, I had realized that my life was too complicated. At the time, I was a cream-and-sugar coffee drinker. I decided to simplify my life with baby steps and start by drinking my coffee black. Yes! "Black," I would smugly say. I drink my coffee black! No super grande mocha coca frappa nonfat organic free-trade soy latte cino for me—no.

Liberated by the simplicity of black coffee, the next year I gave up toxic people. So, three years in a row, revolutionary change: wearing solid clothing, drinking black coffee, no more toxic people. I shudder to think what next year will bring.

Is life as complicated as we make it out to be? As in the pet food aisle, do we really need shelves of books on how to diet, love, grieve, be happy, go green, find a mate, raise small humans?

Sure . . . life is complex—but will complex solutions help? No. Will looking outside ourselves for answers help? No. Will having people tell us *what not to do* help? No. Will looking to gurus help? No. But looking inside will.

The way to solve a complexity is not with more complexity or bar charts or Excel spreadsheets. No. The way to walk into complexity (not solve it) is with local simplicities, simple daily actions—a touch, a smile, a yes, a hug, a voice, a story.

YEAH, I WROTE A DIET BOOK TOO. ONLY FOUR WORDS: **EAT LESS, MOVE MORE.**

And the way to find meaning in our lives, to feel better about ourselves, learn how to navigate relationships, be a better friend, make the Earth more peaceful or green or connected or fun is not by hearing what *not to* do, but by learning and remembering and recognizing what *to* do.

Recently, someone mentioned a new diet book on Twitter, an online social networking site on which you can only communicate using 140 characters at a time. I responded with a short tweet that read: "Yeah, I wrote a diet book too. Only four words: 'Eat less, move more.'"

In writing this book, I kept to my own four-word advice:

Keep it very simple—We're already overwhelmed with complexity. We confuse what is complex (raising a child, finding more meaning in our lives) with what is complicated (sending astronauts to the moon, doing our taxes). Confusing the two leads us to complicated solutions for things that are actually complex instead. No amount of math or newfangled formulas will help you raise a child. Simple wisdom might. As Leonardo da Vinci said, "Simplicity is the ultimate sophistication."

Make them four words—just as writing haiku requires focused attention to a well-defined structure, so will the stricture of four words forge our actions into powerful simplicities. And in a world where I'm bombarded with data and information and spam, perhaps I can remember four important words while I won't remember 50 or 100 or 1,000 words.

Avoid the word "don't"—you won't find "Don't take wooden nickels" or "Don't forget to floss" here. The "direction of intention" in these Zen koans is all positive, moving toward something and not away from it. Not "you could have been," but "you still could be."

Make each an action—you'll find no pronouncements, only actions you can take. It's not useful to hear

wear only
solid clothing

give up

TOXIC

people

that "Life is too short" or "No pain, no gain" or "That's how life is" or "The world is changing." It's more effective to hear some simple actions you can try to make your life richer, simpler, more full.

Like my last book, *Life Is a Verb*, this one is also illustrated with gorgeous original art from around the world by readers of my blog, *37days*. You'll find a list of the artists at the end. What a gift to see how they have interpreted my words visually.

Write your own four-word self-help missives on these pages as you read along. Write the ones that stand out on an index card and carry it with you to the Piggly Wiggly or the Department of Motor Vehicles so you can look at it while you wait. Share them with each other at www.pattidigh.com.

Write in the margins. Make these your own. (See? It's addictive to talk in four-word increments.)

create your own tribe

Some people go to priests; others to poetry;
I to my friends.
—VIRGINIA WOOLF

When my stepfather was dying, his preacher gave me a cell-phone number and told me to call him the moment the end was near, no matter what time of day or night. As Boyce's breathing changed, I stepped outside to dial the number. It was just around 7:00 p.m. on a Sunday night; I knew the preacher was leading a church service at that time, so I just left a message.

Within fifteen minutes, over twenty cars had driven up Boyce's driveway, parking all over the yard at carnival angles, their drivers and occupants coming to the door to hold vigil, pay their respects, straighten up magazines, and just help in the ways we help at those times.

Suddenly the house was full. This is what it means to live in community, I remember thinking to myself. When disaster strikes, when a life ends, your yard fills up with the cars of friends and neighbors. They come bearing casseroles and Jell-O salads with tiny marshmallows in them.

Via the Internet, I have formed a different kind of tribe—one dispersed all over the globe, many of whom I've never met and will likely never meet. Different in circumstance, not in kind. We create our own tribes over time—people we connect to, communities we build, confidences we keep, experiences we share.

Our older daughter, Emma, will graduate soon, leaving behind a group of friends that formed early in her high school years. They affectionately call themselves "The Tribe." Emma's tribe went on a school trip last year and all came back with tattoos. Not knowing how all of the parents would react, they concocted an elaborate scheme of each telling their parents at exactly the same time on exactly the same evening. All of the sets of parental units surprised the girls by not reacting badly. I believe we all looked at those ink trails and experienced a wistful sense of missing those days of solidarity, of shared stories, knowing that when the girls are our age, they will look down at their hip or wrist or ankle and see friendship, pure and simple and amazing.

THE SHORTEST DISTANCE BETWEEN TWO PEOPLE IS A STORY.

The shortest distance between two people is a story. How else do we create a tribe, a community?

other people in

tell them your story

DROP

everything

and **help**

let

someone

help

you

catch
someone
who's falling

surprise them

with presence

mean

what

you

say

walk hand in hand

Hate leaves ugly scars;
love leaves beautiful ones.
—MIGNON MCLAUGHLIN

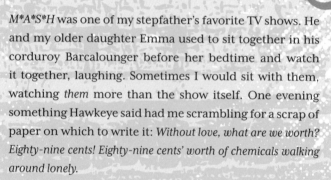

M*A*S*H was one of my stepfather's favorite TV shows. He and my older daughter Emma used to sit together in his corduroy Barcalounger before her bedtime and watch it together, laughing. Sometimes I would sit with them, watching *them* more than the show itself. One evening something Hawkeye said had me scrambling for a scrap of paper on which to write it: *Without love, what are we worth? Eighty-nine cents! Eighty-nine cents' worth of chemicals walking around lonely.*

Eighty-nine cents' worth of chemicals walking around lonely.

Loving is harder than anything else. And more rewarding. Michael Leunig has said, "Love one another and you will be happy. It's as simple and as difficult as that."

Why is love so difficult? Perhaps because we are trying to find love that fits the popular template of what we think love is, much as we try to fit our lumpy bodies into the popular template of what pretty is.

LOVING IS HARDER THAN ANYTHING ELSE. AND MORE REWARDING.

What if we simply walked into the world in a more loving way? What if we learned the difference between loneliness and solitude? What if we approached each situation with one four-word question in our minds and hearts: "What would love do?"

At the end of it all, I know for sure that only love remains. Only love.

SHOW UP.

BE REAL

be
someone
else's
lighthouse

let yourself be
beloved

let yourself be
HURT

embrace solitude,

not loneliness

write more love letters

give someone your

PASSWORD

jump up and down

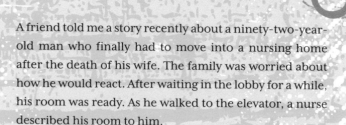

We don't stop playing because we grow old;
we grow old because we stop playing.
—GEORGE BERNARD SHAW

A friend told me a story recently about a ninety-two-year-old man who finally had to move into a nursing home after the death of his wife. The family was worried about how he would react. After waiting in the lobby for a while, his room was ready. As he walked to the elevator, a nurse described his room to him.

"I love it," he said.

"But you haven't seen it yet," the nurse replied.

"It doesn't matter," he responded. "I've decided to be happy ahead of time."

We take ourselves so seriously and our lives often get taken over by stress. Sometimes we just need to play—to reclaim our ability to be happy ahead of time, and to laugh more. As Jean Houston said, "At the height of laughter, the universe is flung into a kaleidoscope of new possibilities."

As we reach adulthood, we're conditioned out of our childlike approach to life, told not to follow our impulses, but to act *appropriately*. What possibilities would open up for us if we forgot that advice and got muddy more often?

SOMETIMES
WE JUST NEED TO
PLAY.

Alan Alda thought of an added bonus to laughing and playing more: "When people are laughing, they're generally not killing each other."

buy experiences,

not things

stop all your

whining

fall down,

get up

GO ON **PLAY** DATES

walk in the woods

play a
childhood
game

be HAPPY
in ADVANCE

take just enough baggage

*A good traveler has no fixed plans,
and is not intent on arriving.*
—LAO TZU

I read a whole book once during a flight to Helsinki, and then reread it on the way home. It was called *Repacking Your Bags: Lighten Your Load for the Rest of Your Life.* In the book, author Richard Leider recalls his experience as host of a safari expedition in Africa, and how he was sporting the latest and best backpack and equipment. He was prepared for any surprise. The Maasai tribal man leading their group kept eyeing the backpack, and finally, after a few days, he asked to see what was in it.

Leider proudly displayed the pack and its contents at the fire one evening. The Maasai man looked at the display, looked at Leider, and then back again. Finally he said the phrase that has stuck with me, all these years later: "Does all that make you happy?"

Seeing the world around us—whether we ever travel on a plane or not—requires being nimble and light, not burdened down. It requires agility to change direction and create our own patterns, to follow our desires and not just the prescribed paths, to be okay with not knowing as we enter the liminal spaces between what we know and what we don't know yet.

It requires us to wander, unencumbered, remembering, as Robert Louis Stevenson once said, "There are no foreign lands. It is the traveler only who is foreign."

SEEING THE WORLD AROUND US REQUIRES BEING NIMBLE AND LIGHT, **NOT BURDENED DOWN.**

explore

your own neighborhood

TALK

TO YOUR

SEATMATES

get off the highway

tip
the hotel maid

find your way home

be your own pilot

leave some things undone

We have all a better guide in ourselves, if we would attend to it, than any other person can be.
—JANE AUSTEN

Not long ago I had dinner with a man named George Renwick. I've known George for years, but this was the first time we had ever sat down together for dinner. We talked and talked. It was the longest dinner I've had in recent history, and we covered much ground. He asked about my book, *Life Is a Verb,* and I talked about the difficulties of continuing to write in the face of all the other things an author does to support a book being born—along with raising a family and running a business. I talked about all my travel and volunteer efforts. I talked about marketing and more. There seemed to be a million pieces to tell. There was a heaviness to the scope of it all.

"Besides your family, what gives you the greatest joy?" he finally asked.

"I am the happiest when I am writing," I said, excitedly describing what it was like when I first started writing my blog, *37days*, in 2005, sitting for hours each day watching words emerge on a screen or on a pad of college-ruled paper. I could physically feel myself lean forward and into the conversation. George listened intently, as George does, his hands crossed in front of him, silent. I spoke for a long time about my passion for writing and the way it makes me feel, my face growing red. Finally I fell silent, thinking about what I had just shared.

BESIDES YOUR FAMILY, WHAT GIVES YOU THE GREATEST JOY?

He asked a single question: "Patti," he said, "what would it take for you to clear your calendar so you could do more writing?"

Sometimes our "stop-doing" list needs to be bigger than our "to-do" list.

STOP

TRYING SO HARD

give up
ITCHY
clothes

let other people drive
other
people
drive

FILL UP YOUR TANK

say
what you can't

TURN OFF
THE SCREEN

LOOK AT THE STARS

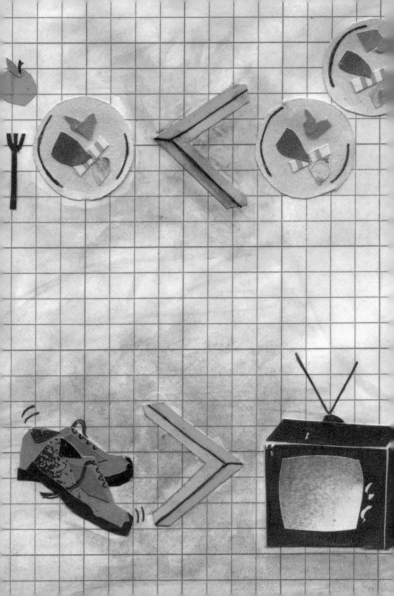

eat less, move more

Be careful about reading health books.
You may die of a misprint.
—MARK TWAIN

In the United States alone, diet aids are a bajillion-dollar business. And yet if we distill all the diet and fitness books down to four words, it might look something like this: "Eat less, move more."

Of course there would be variations on that theme. But fundamentally (for many, but not all of us), it comes down to what we ingest and how much we move around. Simple. Though obviously not simple to do. As Doris Janzen Longacre wrote, "The trouble with simple living is that, though it can be joyful, rich, and creative, it isn't simple."

A few years ago I stopped creating weight goals for myself and started creating "wellness" goals instead. That simple reframing changed everything. The direction of my intention wasn't to be a certain size anymore (a number that is arbitrary and defined by the fashion industry), but to be well—in mind, body, and spirit.

What would committing to wellness look like for you? A ten-minute stretch break or a walk every noontime? A twenty-minute meditation each morning? Finally giving up your addiction to soda? Feeling the sun on your face every day? Or will you share Leslie Grimutter's regimen: "My own prescription for health is less paperwork and more running barefoot through the grass."

WHaT WOULD
COMMITTING
TO WELLNESS
LOOK LIKE
FOR YOU?

Perhaps it is simpler than we think. Maybe Miss Piggy had it just right when she said, "Never eat more than you can lift."

stretch

to stay limber

breathe deeply,
and often

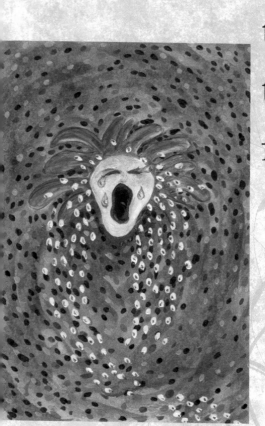

let

the

tears

fall

keep
fresh flowers
nearby

use smaller dinner plates

EAT
MORE
REAL
FOOD

start saying

"I can"

sit in the sunshine

Carol Sloan

do work that matters

One person with passion is better than
forty people merely interested.
—E. M. FORSTER

I had been promoted to vice president very quickly—too quickly (and too young) for the tastes of my fellow vice presidents, I imagine. But there I sat at my very first Board meeting, my four-inch-thick, duly indexed and color-coded Board notebook in front of me, a testament to avoiding surprise.

It was like visiting a foreign country for the first time, what with all the seconding and aye-ing going on. One issue seemed particularly contentious—something about employee parking spaces. It's true that a board can vote to spend $5 million in just ten minutes, but then spend hours on parking spaces or where to hold the holiday party.

The discussion began in earnest and went on for an hour. Finally, someone called the issue to question for a vote. But wait! Another Board member raised issues about whether they needed to vote on the issue, and more discussion ensued.

Suddenly I heard the phrase that made my head pop off my body: "No, we can't vote yet. First we have to *vote on how to vote.*"

I slowly closed my Board book, stood up, and left.

WHERE DOES THE THING ITSELF GO, THAT THING WE ARE WORKING FOR?

Where does the thing itself go, that thing we are working for, the excitement around which we were all centered to begin with? We lose it, plain and simple, in the morass of rules created to keep us out of relationship to each other and to our mission.

Let's reclaim that.

motivate someone

to care

always assume
positive intent

claim your own
mistakes

know what

EXCITES

you

ask why,
not how

DO SOMETHING YOU FEAR

admit
you don't know

start
    handing out
stars

be an earth warrior

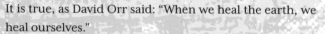

There are no passengers on Spaceship Earth.
We are all crew.
—Marshall McLuhan

It is true, as David Orr said: "When we heal the earth, we heal ourselves."

Years ago, I sat at a business dinner in Sydney, determined not to talk about business. We were among people who actually work to live and not the other way around. I knew that we Americans needed something more than numbers and bar charts and statistics to help us make it through all the dinner courses.

"Let's ask people about the greatest lesson they've ever learned," I had suggested to my husband John as we dressed for dinner. "What's yours?"

And here's what he told me, a tiny story that intrigued all of us later that evening, for its simplicity and truth: "When I was twelve years old at camp, I learned a big lesson from Mr. Overbye, my sixth-grade science teacher. Someone gave me a pair of waders, so I put them on and was stomping around in the middle of a small pond when Mr. Overbye came up to me.

'What are you doing?' he asked me.

'Just playing around,' I answered. 'Just trying out these boots.'

Mr. Overbye stood still and looked at me, silently.

'You are killing more life than you could possibly know,' Mr. Overbye finally said. 'Every step you take, you are destroying whole systems of life.'

we never know how much our behavior can impact **whole ecosystems.**

"It made an impression on me," John told us at dinner. "We never know how much our behavior can impact whole ecosystems. Just one step and I'd wiped out an entire colony. . . ."

The son of one of John's colleagues was killed recently while rock climbing. A renowned climber, Pete Absolon had gone with his friend Steve Herlihy for a challenging climb, but not a serious one. He had a six-year-old daughter at home, and wasn't taking any chances. Right in the middle of a conversation as they climbed, something came hurtling down from above. There was no warning, Herlihy recalled. Just a sudden crack, and then Herlihy saw Pete hanging from the ropes, staring straight ahead. "His face was perfect," Herlihy said, "but I just knew he was dead."

This would be a tragic story even if the rock had simply come loose and fallen on its own. It is all the more tragic because the rock was thrown by someone on the ledge above them. Only after throwing the rock did the young man look over the ledge and see the two men in white helmets, 200 feet beneath him. And at the same moment he registered their presence, the plummeting rock struck Pete directly on the head.

We must see ourselves as part of an intricate ecosystem. Before you wade into the pond, and before you throw that rock, *look over the edge.* Our actions have an impact on other humans, and on the planet.

WATCH
where you
step

TURN OFF

THE LIGHTS

pick up after yourself

GET
YOUR
FINGERNAILS
DIRTY

buy food
from farmers

walk where you can

EAT VEGAN

ON TUESDAYS

stand up for something

On this shrunken globe,
men can no longer live as strangers.
—ADLAI E. STEVENSON

When you stand on the balcony of the Highlander Research and Education Center in New Market, Tennessee, you can see in an instant why these hills are called the Blue Ridge Mountains. Several layers of blue roll in the distance, darker, then lighter, then dark again. Long fields turned ochre and yellow in winter fill the space between you and those hills. My husband John and I recently drove across the mountains to speak to two people at the Center who had fueled the civil rights movement in the United States. Sometimes it is not the folks with the big names who have done the most work; sometimes it is those whose names we don't know.

Our hosts were Guy and Candie Carawan, now in their early eighties. You'll find Guy Carawan's name on sheet music alongside Pete Seeger's. Guy and Candie now live just down the hill from the Center, fifty years after they first met here. It was Guy Carawan who, in 1960, first taught the song "We Shall Overcome" to the founding meeting of the Student Nonviolent Coordinating Committee (SNCC), the group so influential in the civil rights era. "We were asking questions like 'Can we do this with humor or music?', and we just did whatever was needed to make a singing movement. It grew and grew," he said.

That song he taught the SNCC, "We Shall Overcome," is a song of great importance—not only in that place at that time, but in all places and in all times. It is a song whose verses have been sung in many languages around the world, a universal symbol of hope. It is, as John says, one of our greatest exports.

> "We live in such an individualist culture today," she said, but
> ## Great change is communal

Candie continued the story: "In 1959, Guy heard a young man named Reverend Martin Luther King Jr. speak in Boston. Guy was so moved by his words and by the amazing black choir that sang. That's when Guy came to Highlander. We didn't have any freedom songs up until that time. We were using spirituals and hymns and folk songs and love songs, but didn't have any freedom songs. Then Guy taught us 'We Shall Overcome.' Everyone began to rise from their seats, singing and reaching out to join hands, and the signature song of the civil rights movement was born."

"What would you like to teach young people now?" we asked.

It was Candie who answered: "We live in such an individualist culture today," she said, "but great change is communal. The power of song is a vast instrument to draw people together and deliver a message. I think we need to take out our iPod earphones and begin to sing together again."

Great change is communal. Start singing together again. Stand up for something.

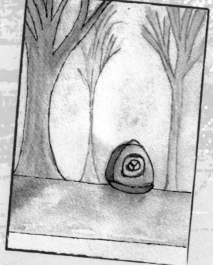

TAKE OUT your earplugs

use

your

own

voice

start a tiny ripple

VOTE
or shut up

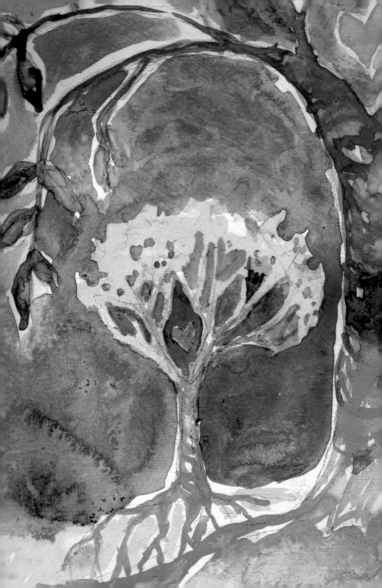

PROTECT

EACH OTHER'S

dignity

speak up
for someone

STOP counting,
START including

earn from small humans

Children make you
want to start life over.
—MUHAMMAD ALI

"Tessie, you wanna go to the creek and take a class?" I asked. I had received a notice for a workshop for five- to seven-year-olds at the Botanical Garden near our house. "YES!" she screamed, unsure of what I was asking but absolutely committed nonetheless. We should all be so sure.

I dropped her off, returning two hours later. The children were creating books about the living things they had seen on their nature walk. The teacher started apologizing in that way adults do, with "asides" above the heads of children. "Well, Tess has quite an imagination," she started, in that way that indicates having quite an imagination is a liability, not an asset. "She is drawing a beach. I told her we should draw what we saw, but she insisted on drawing a beach."

"Well," I said slowly, "Maybe she saw a beach." *Maybe she's five years old and doesn't need to be held to the rigorous standards of the American Botanical Society just yet,* I thought to myself.

The teacher stared at me. "Who knows?" I said playfully, "perhaps that beach is where magic happens!"

"YES!" Tess screamed. "Look! Here's the palm tree I saw!"

The teacher blinked.

I ONLY WISH I SAW
more Fairies
IN MY DAILY LIFE.

I looked down at Tess, happily coloring a palm tree and blue water while her older compatriots labored over spotted spiders and magnolia leaves. And then I saw Tess's scientific notations on her clipboard:

> blueberry
> cicada
> hole
> sstrewbbrry
> waterbug
> nut fish mole

On the "Evidence of Living Things" page, she had joyfully circled poop with a long line of exclamation points after it. As would we all.

A tiny word at the top of Tess's page captured my attention. There, smooshed against the top, was the word fairy.

If she had written in her quivering little hand that she'd seen a fairy and beaches on that walk, far be it from me to argue. I only wish I saw more fairies in my daily life. Perhaps I should try harder. Or maybe I shouldn't try so hard.

We have much to learn from children. They know from Field Day at school that you can't hold a greased watermelon tightly—you have a better chance of keeping it in your arms if you hold it lightly.

Walt Streightiff has said, "There are no seven wonders of the world in the eyes of a child. There are seven million." Like so many fairies. On beaches.

respect who they are

give your affection
freely

talk **WITH**,
not **AT**

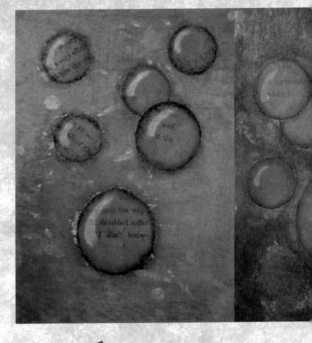

blow bubbles

more
often

SAVE YOUR REFRIGERATOR BOXES

let kids dress
themselves

be a

surge protector

do what you can

Shall we make a new rule of life from tonight:
always to try to be a little kinder than is necessary?
—J. M. BARRIE

In a diner near Philadelphia recently, a couple finished their meal and paid their check. They also paid the check for another table of diners, without telling them. After they left, the waitress told the beneficiaries of the kindness done them. No one knew the couple who had done this act of generosity, but it was a gesture that sparked a whole day of "paying it forward" at that diner. The first beneficiaries left money for another table of diners when they left. That next table left money to pay the bill for yet another table—and so it continued that whole day. The waitresses had never seen anything like it.

Imagine the ripples of small generosities we can spark, all around us—all the time.

The playwright James M. Barrie, whose quote begins this section, is best known as the author of the beloved *Peter Pan*, his most famous work. Rather than keep the profits from that work—millions and millions of dollars by now—Barrie donated all proceeds to the Ormond Street Hospital for Children.

IMAGINE THE RIPPLES OF SMALL GENEROSITIES WE CAN SPARK, ALL AROUND US— **ALL THE TIME.**

Generosity of spirit does show up in the world as financial gifts, but the most significant acts of generosity may be measured only in the way we measure love and kindness—on a scale far from the world of return on investment. A soft word, a special kindness, a silent knowing can all have lasting impact.

Treat people as if they are as fully human as you are (they are). Respect the ideas of people different from you. Offer your last cupcake. Listen fully. These are all acts of generosity, reflections of an overflowing heart. As Erich Fromm has said, "In the act of giving lies the expression of my aliveness."

Express your aliveness by giving—of yourself, of your resources, of your heart.

OPEN DOORS

FOR OTHERS

know what matters
NOW

be kinder than necessary

show up
for someone

try on their shoes

have a
generous
spirit

live like you're dying

Don't let yesterday use up too much of today.
—CHEROKEE PROVERB

It was a death that sparked the writing of my book, *Life Is a Verb*. My stepfather was diagnosed with lung cancer and died just thirty-seven days later. I knew on day 38 that I wanted to live in such a way that when I reached day 1 of my last 37 days, I wouldn't be one of those people who suddenly wanted to drop everything and see the world. I wanted to live a life—a more simple one—so that no matter what number day I was on, I'd wake up and say to myself, "Yes . . . yes. This is exactly the life I wanted."

I recently visited a cemetery in Greensboro, North Carolina, to spend time at the grave of a favorite professor from Guilford College. I hadn't been to the cemetery in fifteen years but knew immediately where Sheridan Simon's distinctive headstone was. I touched the stone, shocked that he had died in 1994, so long ago. He was only forty-six when he died. Forty-six.

The stone that marks his grave is tall and not symmetrical. His name is carved at the bottom; at the top is an engraving that looks like an eclipse or a starburst. Under it are carved these words: THE STARS STILL SHINE.

When told he had a year to live, Sheridan stayed in the classroom, ignoring the advice of his doctors to go see the world, to do what he'd always wanted. He knew where he belonged—with his students, teaching—until seventy-two hours before his death.

LIFE IS incremental.
EACH DAY'S DECISIONS ADD TO THE DECISIONS OF THE DAY BEFORE.

Life is incremental. Each day's decisions add to the decisions of the day before; each action taken adds to the events of the days past. As writer Oscar Wilde has said, "No man is rich enough to buy back his past." No, maybe not. But we can create a different future—one simple, beautifully mundane, daily decision at a time.

How can we live without regret? Perhaps it's not possible. But here are some suggestions for moving in that direction.

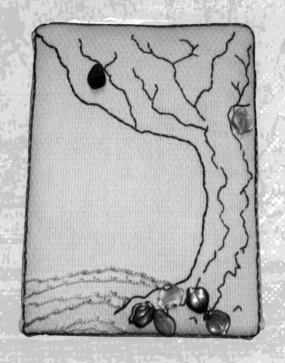

DO LESS,
BE MORE

live life "as if"

RISK
your own significance

seek adventure
AT HOME

get **LOST** more often

in present tense

know it will

END

create your four words

Though there are commonalities that make us all fully human and interconnected, each of us is living a different complexity, aren't we? And so the most important four-word self-help messages *for* you will come *from* you.

What are the four-word self-help messages you need to remember in your own life? Create them here for yourself, or share them with others at www.pattidigh.com:

_____ _____ _____ _____

_____ _____ _____ _____

_____ _____ _____ _____

_____ _____ _____ _____

_____ _____ _____ _____

_____ _____ _____ _____

_____ _____ _____ _____

A writer named Terry Hartley once sent me an essay about changing her verbs. Yes, I thought to myself, that's it. What are the verbs that make up my days? Are they active verbs? Are they fun verbs? Or are they mundane, boring, predictable ones?

Look at the four-word self-help tips you created and notice the verbs. If you don't like them—if they are boring and passive—just change your verbs. Remember the four simple rules as you create your missives:

Keep it very simple.
Make them four words.
Avoid the word "don't."
Make each an action.

One more four-word thought, this one a question that overrides all the others . . .

What would love do?

(Because at the end of it all,
love is what's left.)

meet all the artists

The original art in this book was created by readers of Patti's blog, *37days*.

Page vi Mary Harman, www.maryharmanart.com; page xi Wendee Higa Lee; page xii Laura Allen, www.hungryforlifeblog.com; page xiv Kathryn R. Schuth; page 3 Leah Piken Kolidas, www.BlueTreeArtGallery.com; page 4 Lie Fhung, liefhung.com; page 6 Kathy Iannucci; page 7 Lynne Gillis; page 9 Kathleen Adrian; page 10 Caren S. Knox-Huntley; page 11 Jan Stovall; page 12 Mary Campbell, www.marycampbelldesign.com; page 14 Mary Meares; page 17 Abby M. Nash; page 19 Gwyn Michael, gwynmichael.com; page 20 Eva Miller, www.ncati.org; page 21 Niki Weippert nikisfragments.blogspot.com; page 22 Lisa Call, www.lisacall.com; page 23 Heather Muse; page 25 Paula Bogdan, littlescrapsofmagic.typepad.com; page 26 Cynthia Clack, cynthiaclack.blogspot.com; page 29 Ruth M. Davis; page 30 Elizabeth Bailey, nfluxus.com; page 32 Sherry Smyth, everydaypossibilities.blogspot.com; page 33 Julie Wolkoff; page 34 Andrea Stern, andibeads.blogspot.com; page 37 Tari Goerlitz, www.studiomailbox.com; page 39 Joan Fowler; page 40 Barbara

Kopf Israel; page 43 Barbara D. Holden; Page 45 Patti Tinsman-Schaffer; page 46 Candace Waken; page 48 Kylie Dinning; page 49 Terri J. Johnson, tinkerart.typepad .com; page 51 Cynthia Houck; page 52 Tony Stowers; page 55 Andromeda Jazmon, awrungsponge.blogspot .com; page 57 Andrea Stern, andibeads.blogspot .com; page 60 Cheryl Bakke Martin, inspirations studio.blogspot.com; page 62 Sheryl Nelson, zany.etsy .com; page 63 Karen Starr, karenstarrredesign.com; page 64 Denée Black; page 67 Susie Bertie; page 68 Kristen R. Corlett, www.ttelroc.blogspot.com; page 69 Susan Stone, claudescove.blogspot.com; page 71 Debbie Overton, www.debbieoverton.com; page 74 Paula Kumert, keepitsimplemakeitgreat.blogspot .com; page 75 Carol B. Sloan, carolbsloan.blogspot .com; page 76 Denita Purser; page 79 Susan Nash, www .susans202.com; page 80 Stacey Beth Shulman, www .abundantbliss.net; page 81 Deb Harpster; page 83 Christine Mason Miller, www.christinemasonmiller.com; page 84 Deb Harpster; page 85 Fiona Lucas; page 86 Dawn Meisch, www.dirtykitchen.com; page 87 Kerrie Lee, www.Kerrie-Lee.com; page 88 Susan Kinne; page 92 V. A. Vlach, treedreaming.com; page 93 Sherri Vilov, slvilov .etsy.com; page 95 Peggy Pirro, outofhandart.com; page 96 Debbie Kelley, nourishthesoul.blogspot.com; page 98 Leah Mangue; page 99 Janine King Slaatte; pages

100–101 Elizabeth M. Reynolds, languageofthelens.blog spot.com; page 102 Steven Hoke; page 105 Christy Sobolewski, gulfsprite.com; page 106 Teresa Hartley; page 108 Deb Harpster; page 109 Darcy Thomas; page 110 Kara Brown, www.karabrownlovesart.com; page 112 Tammy Moore, collageobjects.etsy.com; page 113 Christine Martell, christinemartell.com; page 114 Carolie DuBose Brekke, wordmagix.blogspot.com; page 117 Heidi Goldman; page 118 Dana Loffland; page 119 Kathryn R. Schuth; pages 120–121 Angélique Weger, miscellaneaarts .com; page 123 Monica Moran, thecreativebeast.blogspot .com; page 125 Shannon Jackson Arnold, www.theinspired writer.org; page 126 Sylvia Barnowski, fiftytwosteps.blog spot.com; page 129 Amy A. Crawley, amyacrawley.com; page 130 Anne Christ, www.westothemoondesigns.com/ moonlight; page 133 Cheryl Sorg, www.cherylsorg.com; page 134 Kate McGovern, katemcgovernphoto.com; page 135 Julianne Gehan; page 137 Jan Stovall; page 138 Kate Iredale, kateiredale.typepad.com/inspired; page 141 Tresha Barger; page 142 Mary M. Buchanan, threadingthe needle-mary.blogspot.com; page 145 Wendy Cook, www .wendycook.com; page 146 Michelle Doucette Cunningham, www.papercoyote.com; page 147 Linda Bannan; pages 148–149 Marsha Gaspari and Andrew Zizzi, www .boolady.etsy.com; page 151 Maxine Rothman, www .knittingbuddha.com; page 155 Elizabeth Beck, ebeckartist .blogspot.com

always say thank you

In keeping with the simple spirit of this book, just a few four-word thank-yous:

To John, Emma, and Tess Ptak: You are my life. My human survival units.

To Nina McIntosh: Please hold my snake.
To Kathryn Ruth Schuth: You ship really well.
To Amy McCracken: In memory of Eva.
To Kim Joris: Thank you for driving.
To David Robinson: You are so wise.

To my friends on Twitter: Whole worlds in 140.
To teachers everywhere: You so completely rock!
To those who participate in our retreats and workshops: You teach me more.
To all the artists who created beautiful works of art for this book: Your creativity humbles me.

To my editor, Mary Norris: Thanks for your clarity. Thanks for your patience.

who is the author?

Carry your own tuba.
—EMMA PTAK

Do everything you do.
—TESS PTAK

Here's Patti Digh's four-word description of herself: "Most importantly, a mom."

Patti is a writer, speaker, and social justice activist living with her (fantastic, amazing) family—John, Emma, and Tess Ptak—in the mountain town of Asheville, North Carolina. Her last book, *Life Is a Verb: 37 Days to Wake Up, Be Mindful, and Live Intentionally* (skirt! 2008), was a finalist for the Books for a Better Life Award and is beloved by readers around the world. That book can be summed up in these four words: "Live like you're dying." Her new book, *Creative Is a Verb: If You're Alive, You're Creative*, can be distilled to "Life's a creative act."

Patti speaks all over the world about seeing more, living more intentionally, with greater joy, and in deeper community with others.

Be in touch, okay?
Blog: www.37days.com
Web: www.pattidigh.com
Twitter: @pattidigh
Facebook: www.facebook.com/pattidigh
E-mail: patti@pattidigh.com

Patti loves snail mail. Adores it. Mail: P.O. Box 18323, Asheville, NC 28814 USA

© Michael Mauney

ADVICE * why just four words? * k

"don't" * make each an action * d

toxic people * **COMMUNITY** *

space * tell them your story * drop

who's falling * surprise them with

hand * show up, be real * be someo

hurt * embrace solitude, not lonelines

STRESS * jump up and down * buy e

get up * go on play dates * walk in the woods * play

just enough baggage * explore your own neighborh

hotel maid * find your way home * be your own pilo

* give up itchy clothes * let other people drive * fi

look at the stars * **WELLNESS** * eat less, move m

the tears fall * keep fresh flowers nearby * use sma

* sit in the sunshine * **SUCCESS** * do work that m

intent * claim your own mistakes * know what exci

you don't know * start handing out stars * **GREEN**

lights * pick up after yourself * get your fingernails

vegan on Tuesdays * **ACTIVISM** stand up for some

a tiny ripple * vote or shut up * protect each other'

including * **CHILDREN** * learn from small huma

talk with, not at * blow bubbles more often * save

be a surge protector * **GENEROSITY** * do what

matters now * be kinder than necessary * show u

have a generous spirit * **ENDINGS** * live like yo

"as if" * risk your own significance * seek adventure

lost more often * live in present tense * know it wil